Mike Piazza

MIKE AND THE METS

by

Marty Noble

SPORTS PUBLISHING INC.
www.SportsPublishingInc.com

Production manager: Susan M. McKinney
Cover design: Scot Muncaster
Photos: *The Associated Press* and the Albuquerque Dukes

ISBN: 1-58261-051-7
Library of Congress Catalog Card Number: 99-61952

SPORTS PUBLISHING INC.
SportsPublishingInc.com

Printed in the United States.

Contents

Mike batted .348 for the Mets in 1998. (AP/Wide World Photos)

CHAPTER ONE

New Kid in Town

The laws of physics seemingly had been relaxed, like parking rules in Manhattan on a holiday weekend. So when the baseball left the bat of Mike Piazza, it moved like shrapnel leaving a bomb and headed in the general direction of the Gap sign in rightcenter field in Shea Stadium. It wasn't the first ball hit in that direction. It might have been the only one that never slowed down.

Two Brewers outfielders, Marquis Grissom and Jeromy Burnitz, had taken note of the batter and

Mike was traded from Florida to the Mets only a week after the Marlins acquired him from the Dodgers. (AP/ Wide World Photos)

had adjusted their positioning before the newest Met stepped into the batter's box. They were deep and prepared to protect the Gap the way the Broncos protect John Elway. But the baseball sped between them as if propeled by a force greater than the swing of a human. It scraped the Shea lawn more than it bounced off it. Neither Burnitz nor Grissom had a chance to intercept it.

Mike Piazza was going to the wall for the Mets. It was going to be his first hit with the Mets, a run-scoring double in his third at-bat in his first game after his second trade in a week. He had gone from Southern California to south Florida and now he was on his way to second base. Clearly, in all his traveling, he hadn't forgotten to pack his swing.

The double was nothing extraordinary. Mike had hit some harder, others much farther. For the Mets and their fans, however, it was a sign of something special, a calling card from the new man, a demonstration of dominant skill from a player who had joined a team of mostly modest talent.

They all knew the trade had happened, that the best-hitting catcher in the game—perhaps the best ever—had been imported from the Marlins. Now there was on-the-field, in-the-Gap confirmation moving like a bullet toward the wall.

Once the hit was recognized as a bonafide Gapper, the fans roared as they seldom had in recent years. In unison, they delivered a rumbling and extended "Yeah," an echo of the Eighties when the Mets were the best team in the game and Mets fans were full of themselves.

Mike not only had brought out the fans that day in May of 1998, he had brought out something in the fans as well.

CHAPTER TWO

Mike and the Mets

New York is a city of extremes, a city proud of almost any superlative that can be applied. Call New York something that ends with "est"—best, biggest, baddest, loudest, highest, fastest—and the city will thank you. Identify the city as "the most" this or "the least" that and it will be regarded as a compliment. The 1962 Mets were the worst team the game ever has seen, and they were embraced by New York because they were so good at being bad.

On May 22, 1998, when Mike Piazza doubled into the Gap, bruising a pitch from Jeff Juden, he demonstrated he was so good at being good. With a powerful righthanded stroke unlike any other in the game, he appealed to New York's passion for dominance and the extreme. A double rocketed to right center was like a jarring Lawrence Taylor tackle or a biting Dwight Gooden curve ball or a towering Reggie Jackson home run. The very idea of having an ultimate weapon in their arsenal was very appealing to Mets fans.

With Mike Piazza in the Mets' lineup, New York could beat its chest about the Mets again. That was the idea.

The Mets had acquired a durable catcher and a magnificent hitter when they obtained Mike Piazza. They also brought passion back to their ballpark.

"He's making it fun to be a Mets fan again," Nelson Doubleday, one of the Mets' two owners, said a few days after the trade. "Mr. Piazza isn't going to give us just hits and runs—and he's going to give us a lot of those—he's going to make it exciting to be here.

"He gives you a reason to be in your seat when he comes up. He might hit one 150 feet over the wall. You never can tell, the way he swings, he might hit one through the wall. You don't want to miss that."

The Mets fell well short of selling out Mike's debut with the team, but they did sell 9,000 "walk-up" tickets the day of the game, a total significantly higher than the norm. "Mike is an attraction," said Fred Wilpon, Doubleday's partner. "He does have charisma."

After Mike made his Mets debut on the same field where the Beatles, the Rolling Stones and Eric

Mets owners Nelson Doubleday, left, and Fred Wilpon, right, signed Mike to a seven-year, $91-million contract after the 1998 season. (AP/Wide World Photos)

Clapton once performed, he said he felt "like a rock star" because of the reception. He is that kind of attraction. Talented and tall, dominant and dashing, handsome and hard-bodied, well-spoken and well-dressed. Three-piece suits, baseball uniforms and stardom fit him well.

"In this city," Wilpon said, "it doesn't hurt to be a baseball player of Italian descent. . . He could be as big as Willie [Mays] or Mickey [Mantle]." Or the great DiMaggio.

Oh, how the Mets needed that! How they needed a player who almost forces you to take notice, a player with style and flair, a player who makes the uniform fashionable. The Mets had a few in the past—Tom Seaver, Lee Mazzilli, Rusty Staub, Keith Hernandez, Darryl Strawberry, Lenny Dykstra and Gooden. Todd Hundley, traded away in December, was one as well. The Mets believed they needed more to recapture the imagination of the New York market.

They don't compete directly with the Yankees except for those summer days of inter-league play. They certainly do compete with George Steinbrenner's team for the baseball-rich market that once was home to three clubs. Even before the Yankees charged through the 1998 playoffs and World Series, they dominated the market, making the Mets the "other" team in town.

The Mets were as much victims of the Yankees' 1996 World Series championship as the Braves were. The Yankees were a compelling story then, when the relationship of manager Joe Torre and his seriously-ill brother Frank added human interest to baseball excitement. The Mets couldn't compete with that on either level.

The Mets made real improvement in 1997 but fell short of the wild card playoff spot they had aimed to win. So the Yankees stayed ahead. And when they played so well in the first six weeks of the 1998 season, they cast a shadow that denied the Mets all but a few rays of the New York baseball spotlight.

By the time the Dodgers had done the unthinkable and traded Mike Piazza to the Marlins, the Yankees were safely ahead in the American League East race and completely overshadowing the Mets, who were struggling to stay above .500. The Mets had talent and some reasons for hope, but they already trailed the Braves by 9½ games in the National League East. Compared to the Yankees, they were ordinary and a distant second as an attraction.

The addition of Al Leiter, the skilled, handsome and popular lefthanded pitcher, in February, 1998 had been a step toward strengthening the Mets' identity, but it didn't make up for the absence of Hundley, who still was recovering from a serious operation on his elbow.

The acquisition of Michael Joseph Piazza, one of the five premier offensive players in the game; well, that was something else. It gave the Mets the most recognizable baseball name in the New York market, a name known almost everywhere the game is played and a bat feared by any opposing manager.

Even with Paul O'Neill and Bernie Williams playing for the Yankees, the Mets could claim they had the best hitter in the city. Who could argue? Mike is an accomplished hitter with more power than either Yankee. They also could continue to say they had the best catcher in the city, even with Hundley unable to play. Beyond all that, the new man made the Mets a better team.

It was a start.

CHAPTER THREE

Tough Days

As it turned out, it was only a start. The Mets won the first six games following Mike's arrival, extending their winning streak to a season-high nine games. They crushed their opponents in those six games. The weeks that followed were disappointing—to the Mets, their fans and to Mike.

He was hitting, but not like one of the most feared hitters in the game, not like a player who would become the highest paid player in the game five months later, not like a player who had been so

Mark McGwire, left, and Mike, two of baseball's most feared hitters, talk during batting practice before the 1998 All-Star game. (AP/Wide World Photos)

confident in early April that he turned down an offer of $79 million for six years from the Dodgers.

His batting average was acceptable—.308 when he represented the Mets in the All-Star game. He had only 48 RBI, and 35 of the 48 had come with the Dodgers and Marlins. In his brief time with the Mets, there had been "no damage," as the players say. And not enough damage to satisfy the Mets fans who weeks earlier were delighted to welcome him.

Each base runner Mike left in scoring position brought what seemed like thousands of boos. Imagine that, Mike the target of boos. Until he rejected the Dodgers' offer in April, he never had been booed by his home fans.

As much as Mets fans wanted Mike to succeed, they didn't accept his failures. They let him hear their disappointment, sometimes even before he failed.

Mike's lack of RBI became a bigger story to newspapers covering the Mets than the Mets winning and losing. So much of what seemed so right in May seemed so wrong by mid-July. The Mets looked like a so-so team. Instead of being recognized as one of the best hitters in game, Mike was being called a reason for the Mets' disappointing performance.

His lack of production and the way he acted in the clubhouse—he was quiet and rarely smiled—made people think he was unhappy with being a Met. Mike never said he didn't like the big city, but he seemed to act as if he didn't.

Teammates began to wonder about their catcher. Was he unhappy because he wasn't driving in runs or was he not driving in runs because he was unhappy? How much was his contract situation affecting him?

Mike was under contract through the end of the 1998 season. He could become a free agent then and sign a new contract with any club. Players who are about to become free agents often feel extra pressure. They hope to have an especially productive season to increase their value.

The contract Mike had for 1997 and 1998 earned him $15 million. He thought he could make almost as much *per year* in 1999 and thereafter if he performed well in 1998. So there was pressure. He already had rejected the Dodgers' offer for $13.1 million per year.

The Mets hoped to reach a contractual agreement for 1999 and beyond before the end of the season so that Mike never would become a free agent and never receive bids from other clubs. So they began negotiations with Mike's agents, hopeful that an agreement would relieve the pressure he felt.

Mike chases a foul fly ball. (AP/Wide World Photos)

There are no short cuts to negotiating a multi-million dollar contract, however, not one that's fair to each side. Time passed; the pressure didn't. Mike still wasn't producing as had been expected.

Finally in late July, Mets general manager Steve Phillips announced the club and Mike's agents would postpone negotiations until after the season and that Mike and the club would have nothing to say publicly about his contract status until then.

There, the pressure was gone. Or, at least, it was reduced. Mike later admitted the decision by Phillips had helped him deal with it all. It allowed him to direct more of his attention on playing. When he began to produce as had expected, he came to understand it was necessary to separate baseball from business.

"Before I separated things, I was putting too much pressure on myself," Mike said. "It's not like you're thinking about the contract when you're in the batter's box, but you might think of it before the game and it might interfere with batting practice . . . things like that."

Mike also realized he had not been the first player distracted by contract talks. Who could blame him? Hitting a baseball is considered the most difficult task in sports. Concentrating isn't easy with 30,000 fans screaming and with teammates depending on you to be the star. When a fortune is at stake, concentrating isn't any easier.

Mike drove in only eight runs in June. His RBI figure for July was 14. The Mets' team performance reflected problems. The team lost 15 of 27 games in June and 15 of 28 in July. Although they won eight of their last 12 games in July, they finished the month 14 games behind the Braves and behind the Cubs (by four games) and Giants (3½ games) in the competition for the National League wild card playoff berth. The season was getting away from the Mets.

With important contributions from Lenny Harris, Edgardo Alfonzo, John Olerud, Turk Wendell and newly-acquired Tony Phillips, the Mets' season turned around. But no one was more responsible for the about-face than Mike.

The team began a homestand July 28 when manager Bobby Valentine noted that Mike had been hitting but that he "hasn't sizzled like he can." The sizzling began soon after.

In August, Mike hit .347 with eight home runs and 30 RBI. That level of production continued into September—.378, six homers and 22 RBI—as the Mets crept closer to the lead in the race for the wild card.

The U-turn Mike made wasn't the only one. Some Mets fans had begun to believe the hostile greetings Mike had received at Shea Stadium and the regular criticism by radio talk-show callers would persuade him not to re-sign with the Mets. So they did an about face as well.

Mike has become one of the most popular Mets players. (AP/Wide World Photos)

By the end of the season, introductions of "Mike Piazza, No. 31" were met with loud ovations, and his hits led to standing ovations. An internet petition signed by thousands helped to change the last two months of Mike's season and his outlook as well.

After the Mets' final game—a fifth straight defeat, to the Braves in Atlanta, and a runnerup finish in the wild card race—Mike said he had enjoyed his time with the Mets. While he didn't say he would re-sign with them, he didn't say he wouldn't. It was the best news the Mets received during that lost weekend.

Being swept, by the Expos and Braves, in the last two series had left the Mets bitterly disappointed and with a feeling that they had left business unfinished. They were left to think about "what ifs." The biggest one was this: "What if they had Mike Piazza from the beginning of the season?"

If they had had one more victory, they would have tied the Cubs and Giants and forced a three-team playoff for the wild-card spot. Another two victories would have put them in the postseason for the first time since 1988. If Mike had been a Met from March 31 on, would that have been enough?

CHAPTER FOUR

A New Deal

That day in Atlanta, Mike said he had made no decisions about 1999 and beyond. The Mets had made their decision months earlier. They wanted him back. They wanted Mike to be the cornerstone of their lineup and their franchise. Four months and a week hadn't been enough to satisfy them.

During the summer, before Mike had begun to sizzle, there had been private conversations among Mets management. The Mets men had to decide whether it would be wiser to pay a fortune to sign Mike or spend a comparable amount of money to sign two or three other players?

Mike's late push and his overall numbers for the season—a .328 average, 32 home runs, 111 runs batted in, 88 runs, 38 doubles—and his appeal to the fans convinced Doubleday, Wilpon and Phillips that re-signing Mike was essential. Doubleday didn't need to be convinced. He had spoken with Mike in late June during the Mets' three-game series against the Yankees and told him a contract would be worked out if Mike wanted to stay.

Doubleday later admitted his feelings were reinforced by the fans' petition. "We're in the entertainment business," he said. "In entertainment, you listen to your audience. If they like what you give them, you give them more of it."

Doubleday recognized Mike not only as a ballplayer, but also as an investment, a figure the Mets could use in marketing and making the Mets' on-field product appealing to advertisers. Doubleday recalled how, in the Eighties, the Mets had been the hottest show in New York sports, hotter than the Rangers or Islanders, the Knicks or Jets, the Giants who won the Super Bowl three months after the Mets won the World Series. Yes, hotter than the Yankees, too.

Shea Stadium had been the place to be, a place to be seen. As the Mets worked toward contracts for cable television and radio and toward gaining support for a new ballpark, Doubleday and Wilpon wanted to regain that status in the New York sports market. They believed they needed a name to put on the marquee.

Piazza was a good name, a distinctive name. It came with an image—tall, dark and handsome. Thanks to the Mets' generosity, the image came to include rich, too.

Mike congratulates pitcher Al Leiter after a complete-game shutout. (AP/Wide World Photos)

The owners left it up to Phillips, the general manager, to make certain Mike returned. They would provide the finances, Phillips would do the legwork.

There was a sense of urgency involved for Phillips. He knew what his bosses wanted done and he didn't have a lot of time. Because of baseball rules, players who were eligible for free agency couldn't declare themselves free agents until after the World Series and they couldn't negotiate a contract with a different club until two weeks after the Series.

But a player could re-sign with his most recent club at any time. So the Mets had an advantage on other clubs, but they had to move quickly to use it.

They did. They moved so fast, Mike never declared himself a free agent. No other club got a chance to tell Mike what it was willing to invest in him. The Mets made Mike the highest paid player in the history of baseball within a week after the Yankees completed their sweep of the Padres.

Just when the Yankees were supposed to making the most of their World Series championship, the Mets swept in to grab attention of the New York baseball market and all of baseball by signing Mike to a seven-year, $91-million contract.

The back pages of New York's tabloid newspapers belonged to Mike and the Mets. They were the lead story on local television news and on ESPN. The Yankees had just won the World Series, and baseball was talking about Mike and the Mets. That's just what Doubleday and Wilpon had wanted.

Ninety-one million dollars. Wow! The Mets—the whole organization—had been sold for $21.1 million in 1980. The club never had negotiated a contract worth more than $29 million, never had paid one player more than $6.5 million for one season. Mike was going to make an average of $13 million for seven years. Wow!

Mike remained the highest paid player in baseball for less than five weeks. The Angels signed Mo Vaughn and the Diamondbacks signed Randy Johnson for more than $13 million a year. Then the Dodgers signed Kevin Brown for $15 million per year. Mike knew that would happen, and he wasn't complaining.

Neither were the Mets. "The price of playing poker has gone up," Doubleday said. He remembered 1982, the year the Mets signed George Foster for what was then an outrageous amount—$10.2 million for five years. "Doing business in the New York market costs 10 percent more than doing business anywhere else," he said. "But the return is at least that much greater. Look at the Yankees.

"We want to have a team like the Yankees. I'm not saying 'comparable.' I'm saying 'like.' We have to fix our team. And if it costs a lot, it costs a lot. We've learned, maybe the hard way, that we have to put something in before we get something out."

Mike stretches before one of his first games with the Mets. (AP/Wide World Photos)

CHAPTER FIVE

Being the Best

By the time Mike came to New York for the announcement of his signing, everyone in baseball was aware of his contract. He didn't want to dwell on the money. On the day he signed over his future to the Mets, he spoke of passion and intensity, of the growing pains of 1998 and the challenges of 1999. He liked what he saw in front of him, all but admitting he had returned to become the biggest hero in the biggest city.

"LA's great," he said. "But once you come here, you sort of just get infected with the attitude. Going somewhere else now—with no offense to any other place—would just be a letdown. It wouldn't be the same, the same electricity wouldn't be there."

Neither would the challenge be so great, the challenge Mike had created for himself. "I want to be a fixture in New York," he said. "Babe Ruth, Joe DiMaggio, Mickey Mantle . . . Joe Namath . . . Phil Simms. They qualified as New York fixtures. The Yankees teams with Reggie, Thurman Munson, Ron Guidry and Bucky Dent. It's a tremendous legacy."

Mike had thoughts about the Hall of Fame, numbers that suggest he is a legitimate candidate-in-the-making and a plan for how he will dress for a plaque and posterity. "As a Met," he said.

That's what Mike wanted, on top of the $91 million. He didn't aim low. He aimed at New York, vowed to sink his roots in it, and live in it, at least until the first snow. He called New York "the capital of the world." Oh, how New York loved hearing that.

Although he hadn't said so publicly, Mike admitted he knew since the closing weeks of the season that New York was the place. "Why start over?" he said. He never wanted to file for free agency. "What's the sense of filing and seeing what's out there? To me, I really believe I should be here." He called his decision to return "easy."

Mike was asked about the booing of the previous summer. He smiled and said, "Why not be booed by the best?" New York liked that too—the best booers.

His agent, Dan Lozano, said there was "probably more money out there [from another club]." He also said "Mike would like to be to New York what [Frank] Sinatra was."

The Mets hoped it all comes true. "King of the hill. Top of the heap. A-number 1" and all that.

They wanted Mike to be a part of it. They expected he would be the biggest part. That's why Doubleday and Wilpon were willing to pay Mike $79 million more for seven years than they paid all the Mets who produced the 1986 World Series championship.

"As I have done with all my contracts," Mike said, "I'd like to make it seem like a bargain."

CHAPTER SIX

By the Numbers

In baseball, it always comes down to numbers. Numbers—statistics—are the language of the game: 20-game winners, .300 hitters, 60, 61, 66 and now 70 home runs. A 56-game hitting streak, the last .400 hitter, 20 strikeouts in one game, 40-40 men and 2,621 consecutive games played. Some numbers are as recognizable as the names of the players who produce them.

For Mike Piazza, there are all sorts of numbers: his .333 career average and 200 career home runs tell us what he has done; his new contract—

Mike crosses the plate after his first grand slam home run as a Met. (AP/Wide World Photos)

seven years and $91 million—tells us what his value is and the numbers 62 and 1,389 tell us where he came from and what he had to overcome to reach another number—his rank among catchers.

He is regarded as the No. 1 offensive catcher in the game today; an argument can be made that he is the best hitting catcher ever. And, according to research by the Elias Sports Bureau, Mike already has achieved a special place in baseball.

When he hit his 26th home run in 1998, he increased his career totals for hits and home runs to 1,000 and 194 and increased his career batting average to .330. Only Babe Ruth had a higher average (.345) *and* more home runs (229) within his first 1,000 hits.

Numbers don't tell the entire story about the Mets catcher; however they do provide some insight into who he was, who he is and what he may become.

When the Dodgers drafted Mike, they did so as a favor to Tommy Lasorda. (AP/Wide World Photos)

Mike was selected by the Dodgers in the 62nd round of baseball's amateur draft in 1988. He was chosen after 1,389 others. Imagine that. There were 26 clubs in baseball in 1988, and not one of them thought enough of the 19-year-old kid from Norristown, Pennsylvania, to select Mike in the first 61 rounds. Twenty-six teams thought there were 1,389 other amateur players with more ability and better chances to reach the big leagues than Mike.

Considering where he is today, considering that he is compared with Hall of Fame catchers Johnny Bench, Yogi Berra and Roy Campanella, and is mentioned in the same breath as Ruth, it seems impossible Mike didn't show more promise in 1988 or that no one noticed the promise he did show.

Even when the Dodgers finally did draft him, they did so as a favor to Tommy Lasorda, their long-time manager and a long-time, close friend of Mike's father Vince.

The organization had so little genuine interest in Mike that it didn't even contact him until a month after the draft.

Finally, Vince Piazza telephoned Lasorda, his friend, to see what had happened. The manager had his friend's son fly to Los Angeles for an after-the-draft audition. Lasorda made arrangements to have Mike work out in Dodger Stadium.

Lasorda, a wonderful story-teller, loves to tell this story in particular:

"I made Mike work out for the scouting director [Ben Wade]," he said. "And he put on a pretty good show in batting practice. So Wade says 'Get his schedule for me, and I'll go back and see him play.'

"I said if he was a shortstop, wouldn't you try to sign him right now?" Lasorda asked, knowing how unusual it was find a shorstop with offensive skills.

And Wade said "Sure, if he was a shortstop I'd sign him right now."

"Well, what if he was a catcher?" Lasorda said, knowing good-hitting catchers also are rare. "Would you sign him then?"

Wade said "Well, if he were a catcher, yeah."

So Lasorda said "'Then he's a catcher. Sign him.' And that's what they did." The first contract Mike signed to play baseball earned him $15,000.

Mike throws to first for a double play. (AP/Wide World Photos)

CHAPTER SEVEN

Challenges

The problem was that Mike had never been a catcher. He was a first baseman. And you just don't decide, "Okay, I think I'll become a catcher today." It is the game's most demanding position and it takes the longest to master.

Lasorda knew his friend's son was willing to learn and willing to work, willing to do whatever was necessary to become a major league player. If it meant Mike would have to shift to the game's most difficult position, well. . .he would do it.

Lasorda had Mike assigned to the Dodgers' winter camp in the Dominican Republic. Mike would learn to catch there. It would be a real crash course.

Mike was the only player in camp who spoke English. So he learned a new position and parts of a new language. It wasn't easy. He wasn't yet the muscled, 215-pound player he is today. He was 6-3 and 200 pounds then with a body that hardly was suited for catching. Mike lacked quickness and technique. Only technique can be learned.

With a work ethic that made others sweat, Mike worked to learn his new position and to polish the offensive skills that had caught the eyes of Lasorda, Wade and others.

There never has been a question about Mike's willingness to work at his trade. His work ethic is second to none. He got it from his father, a self-made millionaire.

Vince Piazza left high school at age 16 to work full-time to support his family. He eventually purchased a used-car lot with money he had earned repairing cars. That lot was one of many he owned by the time Mike and his four brothers were young adults. Vince's small empire was valued at more than Mike's most recent contract—about $100 million.

With the support of his father, Mike worked as tirelessly at baseball as Vince had as a teenager. When Mike was 12 years old, Vince built a batting cage in the backyard of the family home and then waited for complaints from his neighbors.

As Mike's father tells the story, the building inspector did wonder about the oddly-shaped, plywood "thing" in the Piazza's backyard.

"That's my son's ticket to the major leagues," Vince told anyone who would inquire.

Swings in the cage became a regular part of Mike's life, even during Pennsylvania winters. If snow had to be shoveled, he'd do it.

"On the bad-weather days, my father would tell me 'Ya know, the kids in California are taking batting practice today,'" Mike says now. "He didn't really push me that much, but he let me know how much could be accomplished—in anything, not just baseball—if you worked at it.

"I'm not afraid to work at something. I like challenges."

He said the challenge of helping to push the Mets into the postseason was one of the things that made Mike decide to return to the Mets.

"Mike had hoped he could be the player who drove the Mets into the playoffs last year," his agent Dan Lozano said the day Mike re-signed with the team. "He was very disappointed. Now that's even more important to him because they didn't get in. He likes the challenge.

"Remember, this is a guy who wasn't taken until the 62nd round, a guy who never caught a game in his life. And now he's a star. You have to know he likes challenges."

Mike has always been a good hitter, but after being signed by the Dodgers he had to learn to play a new position—catcher. (AP/Wide World Photos)

CHAPTER EIGHT

The Hitter

There is no question, Mike made it to the big leagues as a hitter, not as a catcher. But what a hitter!

He wasn't always a great hitter. The statistics he produced in his first two seasons after signing with the Dodgers were not extraordinary, but were good enough to persuade the Dodgers to promote him to the next level of the minor leagues.

He led the Dodgers' minor leaguers in home runs, with 29, in 1991. Only three players in all of minor league baseball hit more that season.

Mike spent part of 1992 with the Triple A Albuquerque Dukes. (Albuquerque Dukes)

In 1992, after Mike was assigned to the Dodgers' San Antonio affiliate in the Double A Texas League, he exploded, batting .377 with seven home runs in only 114 at-bats. Promotion to the Albuquerque, New Mexico, team in the Triple A Pacific Coast League followed; so did more productive hitting.

Mike batted .341 in 358 at-bats with the organization's best minor league team and almost forced the Dodgers to promote him to the major leagues. He made his major league debut September 1 against the Cubs in Chicago with three hits and a walk.

He didn't crush major league pitching in that brief, one-month tenure—only 69 at-bats. But Lasorda and his coaches had seen enough in spring training and heard enough from Albuquerque. Mike was set to be the Dodgers' regular catcher in 1993.

Mike looks down at the ball after two runs were scored. (AP/Wide World Photos)

Mike wasn't ready for the major leagues—not as a catcher anyway. As a hitter he was fully prepared, as his production proved. He went on to be the National League Rookie of the Year that season because of his hitting.

He still isn't the best defensive catcher in the game. These days, that distinction goes to either Charles Johnson of the Orioles or Ivan Rodriguez of the Rangers. In fact, during Mike's time with the Dodgers, there were criticisms—some whispered, some shouted—from some pitchers about his work behind the plate.

Those criticisms never were heard when Mike hit the three-run home run that spared the pitcher from a defeat or when he blocked the plate—as he does so willingly to deny an opponent a run.

The Mets pitchers didn't complain last season. Those who were there long enough knew what it was like to have a power-hitting catcher. Todd

Hundley had hit 41 home runs in 1996 and 30 in 1997 before his elbow betrayed him. And the Mets catchers—Alberto Castillo, Tim Spehr, Jim Tatum, Rick Wilkins and Todd Pratt—didn't hit much in the first six weeks of the season.

When Mike arrived, the pitchers found few problems they couldn't deal with. By the end of the 1998 season, the Mets' earned run average was 3.91 with Mike catching and 3.55 with the others, a difference of less than half a run.

Only the Braves catchers outproduced the Mets' catchers, and Mike caught in only 99 of the Mets' 162 games. No pitcher was going to complain. Mike has made himself into an adequate catcher.

CHAPTER NINE

The Catcher

Nothing wears down a player like catching. Even if there were no foul tips bouncing off his unprotected right hand or his shoulder, no blocking the plate, no hurried off-balance throws and no dugout steps or walls to contend with, catching still would be the most demanding position on the field. It is both mentally and physically challenging.

Even a pitcher who throws 130 pitches in a complete game is not likely to expend the energy his catcher does—squatting, backing up first base

Mike and John Olerud congratulate each other after a Mets win. (AP/Wide World Photos)

and just returning the ball to the pitcher. These days, pitchers rarely work nine innings. Catchers do, especially catchers who hit the way Mike hits.

Pitchers always worry about their arms—at least they ought to. Most position players take throwing for granted. What 18-year-old catcher thinks twice about tossing the ball back to the pitcher? It's not more strenuous than walking back to the huddle in football

But when you can't throw, well. . .

When Todd Hundley was working to come back from his serious elbow surgery in 1998, his elbow would allow him to complete the drills the doctors and trainers had prescribed. But he wondered about the strain of throwing the ball back to the pitcher. If he were to catch all nine innings and, say, 130 pitches, and return the ball to the pitcher eight times before each inning, he could make as many as 200 throws.

Mike tags out Fernando Seguignoi of the Montreal Expos. (AP/Wide World Photos)

Now factor in foul tips, the collisions, the steps, the possibility of getting hit by a a batter's back swing or a follow-through—that happened to Mike a few times last season.

"That's why you 'play' shortstop and you 'play' the outfield or first base," Yankees manager Joe Torre says. "But no one ever says you 'play' catcher. It's too much like work." Torre broke into the major leagues as a catcher.

Bill Russell, Mike's last manager with the Dodgers, says catching might be the least appreciated and understood position in the game.

"By the All-Star break, you can't find a catcher who's fresh or not banged up," Russell says. "There aren't any. They get hit by pitches and bats and foul balls. They block the plate, throw from impossible positions. To do all that and still hit like Mike does? It's amazing."

Mike felt like a target at times during his first tour with the Mets. He was hit by a pitch on the back of the left hand by Pedro Martinez, his one-time teammate, in Fenway Park June 6. He was struck on the left side of his skull by the follow through of a swing by Gerald Williams July 4. There were other typically catcher bruises he had to endure on a daily basis.

Yet he appeared in all but nine of the Mets' games after his arrival May 23, catching in 100 of them. Mike also started 41 games with the Dodgers and Marlins, so he was the starting catcher in 140 games. Only Jason Kendall of the Pirates started more games (143) than Mike, and only Kendall (1,253⅓) and Ivan Rodriguez of the Rangers (1,197⅓) caught more innings than Mike (1,190).

A very ambitious off-season training progam and a strong body enable Mike to deal with the injuries and the fatigue.

"You have to be strong from the first day," he says. "You can't get stronger during the season because the games just wear you down. The best you can hope to do is stay even, stay where you are when the season started. But that doesn't happen when the hot weather comes."

Playing in New York, which is considerably more humid than Los Angeles, could sap Mike of some of his stength too. But, having grown up on the East Coast, and having played in Miami, Atlanta and St. Louis, he was accustomed to the humidity and maintained his stength.

In fact, Mike played as much as he did despite the preference of Mets manager Bobby Valentine to rest his players. Only Mets first baseman John Olerud played more regularly than Piazza last summer. Valentine monitored them closely to make sure they weren't overdoing it.

Valentine, a close friend of Lasorda, consulted with the former Dodgers manager about Mike. Mike played in 149 games in 1993 and 148 in 1996 with Lasorda managing and 152 in 1997 when Lasorda and Russell were the Dodgers' managers. The two years in which Mike played fewer than 140 games were 1994 and 1995 when the baseball seasons were shortened by the player's strike.

CHAPTER TEN

10

Proving Himself

Watch closely someday as Mike walks to the plate or back from the mound. You might notice a slight limp. Ted Simmons, the former Cardinals catcher, calls it "the catcher's gait." It's an occupational hazzard, much the same as the dropped shoulder you may noticed on a veteran power pitcher.

Almost every catcher limps—even the younger ones. That's why people often ask Mike why he continues to catch. Why not change positions? Move to third base. Joe Torre and Johnny Bench did. Todd Zeile, Mike's good buddy from the Dodgers (they were Marlins teammates for a week before Mike was traded to the Mets), changed from catcher to third base when he was with the Cardinals. Two-time Most Valuable Player Dale Murphy moved from catcher to center field. Craig Biggio switched from catching to play second base.

In each case, the idea was to reduce the strain on the legs—mostly the knees—of a quality hitter. The idea was to prolong the player's career.

Mike's been asked about changing positions too. That possibility came up after Mike had joined the Mets and Hundley was ready to come back from his elbow surgery. Mike said he was willing to try, but most people thought he wanted to stay behind the plate.

"I've worked so hard to learn to catch, I want to continue catching," he said in the summer of 1997, days before he served as the National League starting All-Star catcher for the fourth straight year. He also started in 1998 when he represented the Mets.

"I can understand the way Mike feels," Lasorda said in July 1997. "Mike went through a lot to learn the position. He worked as hard as you can work. Now he's at a point where he could go down in history as one of the greatest—if not the greatest—hitting catchers of all time.

"I can understand it if he want to stay back there."

"Obviously," Mike says, "catching is a very physically demanding position, and I love my catching. It's not an easy decision. To make a move just to move a guy, you're going to be a liability [at a new position] for a while because you're not going to have the experience."

Besides, changing positions would be too much like quitting. That's one thing Mike doesn't do very well.

He did once in 1990 after a game in the Florida State League. He told the Vero Beach Dodgers he was quitting. Mike had grown tired of hearing that his place in the Dodgers organization had been given to him by Lasorda. Vero Beach manager Joe Alvarez had made comments about the Piazza-Lasorda relationship and began to platoon a lesser hitter/better catcher, Pete Gonzalez, with Mike.

"I regret the situation ever happened," Mike says. "It wasn't a low point. I was just deciding to move on with my life. I wasn't having fun playing baseball. I wasn't playing, and I wasn't having fun sitting on the bench. I said, 'Hey, I gave it a good shot. I played professionally, not a lot of guys get a chance to say that.' Looking back, if things would have occurred the same way, I probably would have done the same thing."

Mike talked it over with Lasorda, his father and the Dodgers' front office and returned after four days. His return and work ethic eventually brought the team closer together.

Mike still heard the accusations even after he had established himself as a major league star. By the end of the 1997 season, he had produced three seasons of more than 100 RBI, five seasons with batting averages of .318 to .362 and four seasons with at least 32 home runs. "And I still keep hearing how my dad pulled strings to get me in, how Tommy put me on the team because of his friendship with my father," Mike says. "What? I don't belong? I haven't done enough to prove I deserve to be here?"

Mike's bat breaks during a swing in 1998. (AP/Wide World Photos)

CHAPTER ELEVEN

11

Looking Ahead

Of course Mike had proved himself. He did enough each year between 1993 and 1997 to place among the top 10 in the balloting for the National League MVP Award. He placed second in 1996 and 1997, fourth in 1995, sixth in 1994 and ninth in 1993, the year he was the unanimous choice as the league's Rookie of the Year.

Even in 1998, when he played with three teams and missed the Mets' first 44 games, he placed 14th in the MVP balloting. His father and Lasorda had nothing to do with the voting.

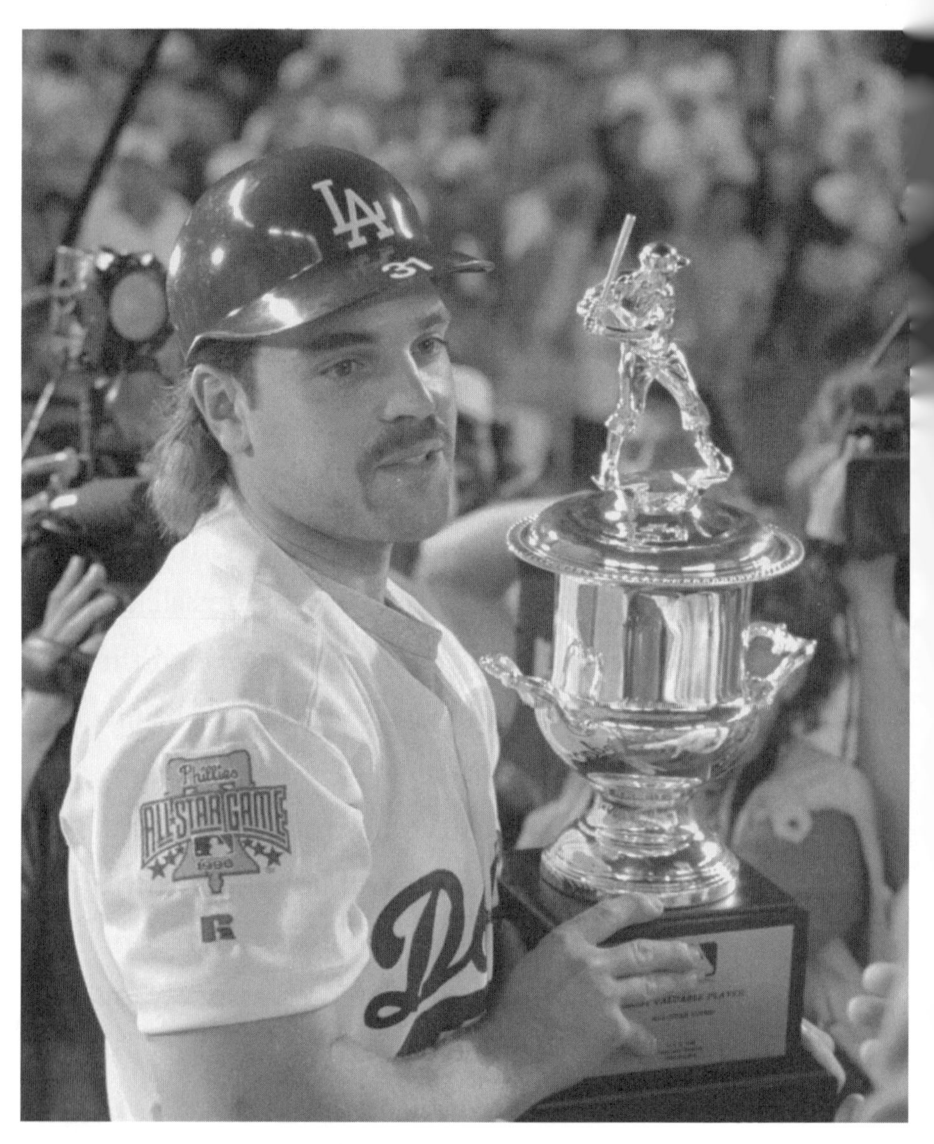

Piazza was named the MVP of the 1996 All-Star Game. (AP/Wide World Photos)

Nor did they make Mike the leading vote-getter in the All-Star balloting in 1996 and 1997 or the All-Star Game MVP in 1996 or enable him to bat .362 in 1997. That year he came within 11 points of becoming the first catcher to lead the league in batting since 1942, when Ernie Lombardi did it.

Yet for all he has accomplished as a hitter and all the work he has done to make himself the catcher he is, he has maintained a sense of where he fits in the game. Induction into baseball's Hall of Fame may be his future. But for now he remains modest. He was asked to pose with Bench and Roy Campanella a few years back and declined, saying, "I don't see myself in their class. They did it for their whole careers. If I did what I'm doing now for a few more years, maybe then it will be appropriate. Not yet."

Mike has a career batting average of .333.
(AP/Wide World Photos)

A player must play 10 seasons in the major leagues to be eligible for the Hall of Fame. If Mike produces for four more seasons as he has in the first six—107 RBI, 33 home runs, 85 runs and .333 average, he would almost be assured of election, even if he changes positions.

The Mets hope he continues for another seven seasons.

After that, who knows? Mike will turn 37 late in the 2005 season. These days players extend their careers beyond their 40th birthday far more than they ever have. But Mike has other areas that interest him.

He has made cameo appearances on "Married With Children," "Baywatch," "The Bold and The Beautiful" and on MTV. Broadcasting appeals to him as well. "There are other horizons," Mike says.

As Mike said on the final day of the Mets' 1998 season, "There is unfinished business here." There is room in his scrapbook for more highlights. Winning the All-Star Game MVP in a game in Philadelphia, so close to his Norristown, Pennsylvania, home, was a thrill. Carving himself a place in the game near Bench, Ruth and Campanella was special too.

But Mike has never played in a World Series. The Dodgers teams he played with lost all six postseason games they played. Reaching the World Series is a challenge. But then, so was being drafted in the 62nd round.

Mike Piazza Quick Facts

Full Name: Michael Joseph Piazza
Team: New York Mets
Hometown: Norristown, Pennsylvania
Position: Catcher
Jersey Number: 31
Bats: Right
Throws: Right
Height: 6-3
Weight: 215 pounds
Birthdate: September 4, 1968

1998 Highlight: Batted .348 with 23 homers and 76 RBI in 109 games with the Mets.

Stats Spotlight: His .333 career batting average ranks second to only Tony Gwynn among active players.

Little-Known Fact: Mike was the 1,390th player chosen in baseball's 1988 amateur draft.

Mike Piazza's Major League Career

Year	Club	AVG	G	AB	R	H	2B	3B	HR	RBI	BB	SO	SB
1992	Los Angeles	.232	21	69	5	16	3	0	1	7	4	12	0
1993	Los Angeles	.318	149	547	81	174	24	2	35	112	46	86	3
1994	Los Angeles	.319	107	405	64	129	18	0	24	92	33	65	1
1995	Los Angeles	.346	112	434	82	150	17	0	32	93	39	80	1
1996	Los Angeles	.336	148	547	87	184	16	0	36	105	81	93	0
1997	Los Angeles	.362	152	556	104	201	32	1	40	124	69	77	5
1998	Los Angeles	.282	37	149	20	42	5	0	9	30	11	27	0
	Florida	.278	5	18	1	5	0	1	0	5	0	0	0
	New York	.348	109	394	67	137	33	0	23	76	47	53	1
	M.L. Totals	.333	840	3119	511	1038	148	4	200	644	330	493	11

Active Career BA Leaders

Tony Gwynn	.339
Mike Piazza	**.333**
Wade Boggs	.329
Frank Thomas	.321
Edgar Martinez	.318
Alex Rodriguez	.313
Kenny Lofton	.311
Rusty Greer	.310
Mark Grace	.310
Nomar Garciaparra	.309

Active Career Slugging Percentage Leaders

Frank Thomas	.584
Albert Belle	.577
Mark McGwire	.576
Mike Piazza	**.575**
Ken Griffey Jr.	.568
Juan Gonzalez	.568
Manny Ramirez	.558
Barry Bonds	.556
Nomar Garciaparra	.552
Larry Walker	.552

Active Career AB/HR Leaders

Mark McGwire	11.2
Juan Gonzalez	14.2
Albert Belle	14.6
Ken Griffey Jr.	14.9
Jose Canseco	15.2
Frank Thomas	15.4
Mike Piazza	**15.6**
Jim Thome	15.8
Barry Bonds	16.1
Cecil Fielder	16.2

Active Career AB/RBI Leaders

Juan Gonzalez	4.5
Mark McGwire	4.5
Frank Thomas	4.6
Albert Belle	4.6
Mike Piazza	**4.8**
Manny Ramirez	4.9
Jose Canseco	5.0
Jeff Bagwell	5.0
Matt Stairs	5.0
Mo Vaughn	5.1

1998 NL Hits Leaders

1.	Dante Bichette	219
2.	Craig Biggio	210
3.	Vinny Castilla	206
4.	Vladimir Guerrero	202
5.	Derek Bell	198
6.	Sammy Sosa	198
7.	Fernando Vina	198
8.	John Olerud	197
9.	Jeff Cirillo	194
10.	Doug Glanville	189
14.	**Mike Piazza**	**184**

1998 NL BA Leaders

1.	Larry Walker	.363
2.	John Olerud	.354
3.	Dante Bichette	.331
4.	**Mike Piazza**	**.328**
5.	Jason Kendall	.327
6.	Craig Biggio	.325
7.	Vladimir Guerrero	.324
8.	Jeff Cirillo	.321
9.	Tony Gwynn	.321
10.	Vinny Castilla	.319

1998 NL Home Run Leaders

1.	Mark McGwire	70
2.	Sammy Sosa	66
3.	Greg Vaughn	50
4.	Vinny Castilla	46
5.	Andres Galarraga	44
6.	Moises Alou	38
7.	Jeromy Burnitz	38
8.	Vladimir Guerrero	38
9.	Barry Bonds	37
10.	Jeff Bagwell	34
13.	**Mike Piazza**	**32**

1998 NL RBI Leaders

1.	Sammy Sosa	158
2.	Mark McGwire	147
3.	Vinny Castilla	144
4.	Jeff Kent	128
5.	Jeromy Burnitz	125
6.	Moises Alou	124
7.	Dante Bichette	122
8.	Barry Bonds	122
9.	Andres Galarraga	121
10.	Greg Vaughn	119
12.	**Mike Piazza**	**111**

Derek Jeter: The Yankee Kid

Author: Jack O'Connell

ISBN: 1-58261-043-6

In 1996 Derek burst onto the scene as one of the most promising young shortstops to hit the big leagues in a long time. His hitting prowess and ability to turn the double play have definitely fulfilled the early predictions of greatness.

A native of Kalamazoo, MI, Jeter has remained well grounded. He patiently signs autographs and takes time to talk to the young fans who will be eager to read more about him in this book.

Bernie Williams: Quiet Superstar

Author: Kevin Kernan

ISBN: 1-58261-044-4

Bernie Williams, a guitar-strumming native of Puerto Rico, is not only popular with his teammates, but is considered by top team officials to be the heir to DiMaggio and Mantle fame.

He draws frequent comparisons to Roberto Clemente, perhaps the greatest player ever from Puerto Rico. Like Clemente, Williams is humble, unassuming, and carries himself with quiet dignity. Also like Clemente, he plays with rare determination and a special elegance. He's married, and serves as a role model not only for his three children, but for his young fans here and in Puerto Rico.

Ken Griffey, Jr.: The Home Run Kid

Author: Larry Stone

ISBN: 1-58261-041-x

Capable of hitting majestic home runs, making breathtaking catches, and speeding around the bases to beat the tag by a split second, Ken Griffey, Jr. is baseball's Michael Jordan. Amazingly, Ken reached the Major Leagues at age 19, made his first All-Star team at 20, and produced his first 100 RBI season at 21.

The son of Ken Griffey, Sr., Ken is part of the only father-son combination to play in the same outfield together in the same game, and, like Barry Bonds, he's a famous son who turned out to be a better player than his father.

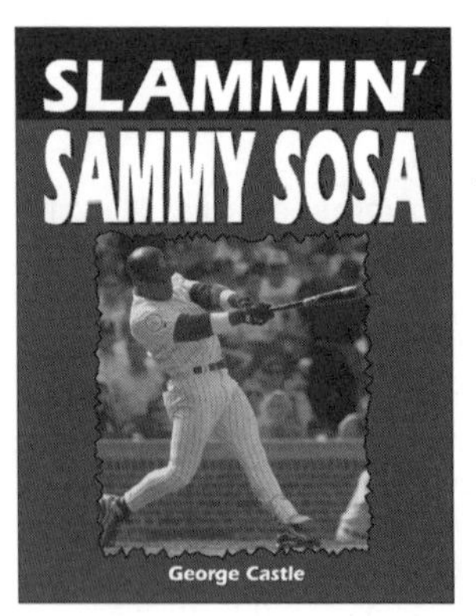

Sammy Sosa: Slammin' Sammy

Author: George Castle

ISBN: 1-58261-029-0

1998 was a break-out year for Sammy as he amassed 66 home runs, led the Chicago Cubs into the playoffs and finished the year with baseball's ultimate individual honor, MVP.

When the national spotlight was shone on Sammy during his home run chase with Mark McGwire, America got to see what a special person he is. His infectious good humor and kind heart have made him a role model across the country.

Mark Grace: Winning with Grace

Author: Barry Rozner

ISBN: 1-58261-056-8

This southern California native and San Diego State alumnus has been playing baseball in the windy city for nearly fifteen years. Apparently the cold hasn't affected his game. Mark is an all-around player who can hit to all fields and play great defense.

Mark's outgoing personality has allowed him to evolve into one of Chicago's favorite sons. He is also community minded and some of his favorite charities include the Leukemia Society of America and Easter Seals.

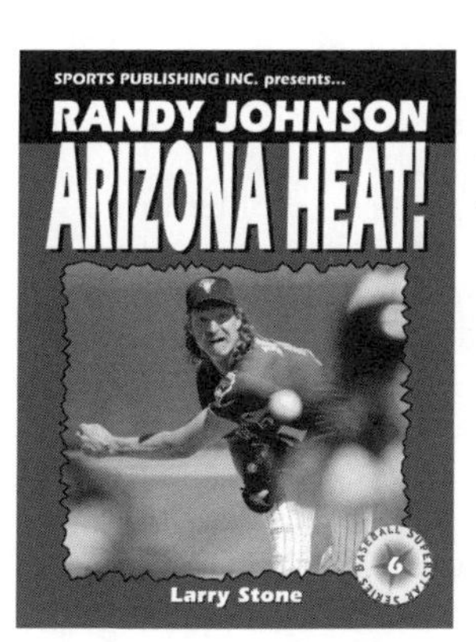

Randy Johnson: Arizona Heat!

Author: Larry Stone

ISBN: 1-58261-042-8

One of the hardest throwing pitchers in the Major Leagues, and, at 6'10" the tallest, the towering figure of Randy Johnson on the mound is an imposing sight which strikes fear into the hearts of even the most determined opposing batters.

Perhaps the most amazing thing about Randy is his consistency in recording strikeouts. He is one of only four pitchers to lead the league in strikeouts for four consecutive seasons. With his recent signing with the Diamondbacks, his career has been rejuvenated and he shows no signs of slowing down.

Mo Vaughn: Angel on a Mission

Author: Mike Shalin

ISBN: 1-58261-046-0

Growing up in Connecticut, this Angels slugger learned the difference between right and wrong and the value of honesty and integrity from his parents early on, lessons that have stayed with him his whole life.

This former American League MVP was so active in Boston charities and youth programs that he quickly became one of the most popular players ever to don the Red Sox uniform.

Mo will be a welcome addition to the Angels line-up and the Anaheim community.

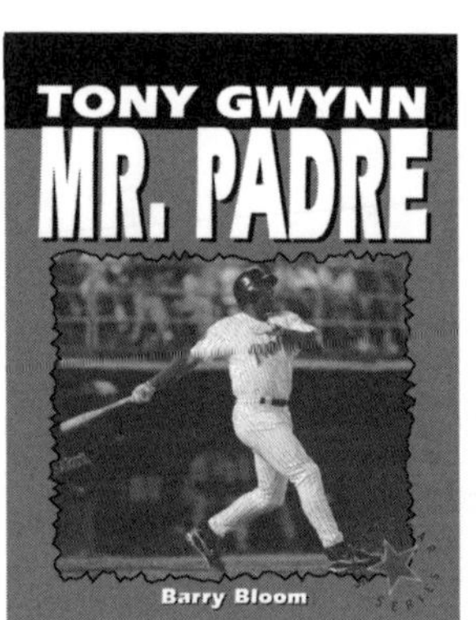

Tony Gwynn: Mr. Padre

Author: Barry Bloom

ISBN: 1-58261-049-5

Tony is regarded as one of the greatest hitters of all-time. He is one of only three hitters in baseball history to win eight batting titles (the others: Ty Cobb and Honus Wagner).

In 1995 he won the Branch Rickey Award for Community Service by a major leaguer. He is unfailingly humble and always accessible, and he holds the game in deep respect. A throwback to an earlier era, Gwynn makes hitting look effortless, but no one works harder at his craft.

Curt Schilling: Phillie Phire!

Author: Paul Hagen
ISBN: 1-58261-055-x

Born in Anchorage, Alaska, Schilling has found a warm reception from the Philadelphia Phillies faithful. He has amassed 300+ strikeouts in the past two seasons and even holds the National League record for most strikeouts by a right handed pitcher at 319.

This book tells of the difficulties Curt faced being traded several times as a young player, and how he has been able to deal with off-the-field problems.

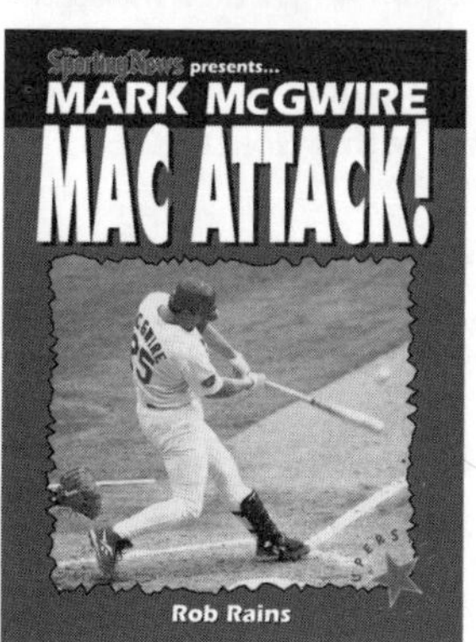

Mark McGwire: Mac Attack!

Author: Rob Rains
ISBN: 1-58261-004-5

Mac Attack! describes how McGwire overcame poor eyesight and various injuries to become one of the most revered hitters in baseball today. He quickly has become a legendary figure in St. Louis, the home to baseball legends such as Stan Musial, Lou Brock, Bob Gibson, Red Schoendienst and Ozzie Smith. McGwire thought about being a police officer growing up, but he hit a home run in his first Little League at-bat and the rest is history.

Roger Clemens: Rocket Man!

Author: Kevin Kernan
ISBN: 1-58261-128-9

Alex Rodriguez: A-plus Shortstop

ISBN: 1-58261-104-1